Praise for _Twinings_

"Julie Fritz's poetry is a wonder of economy, beauty, and deep thoughtfulness. She takes small, simple things and reveals their complexity. Best of all, she takes you along as a friend pointing out things that you wouldn't have known you knew unless she had been there to remind you. _Twinings_ is delightful in every important way."

—Phyllis Theroux, author of
The Journal Keeper

"Wistful and wise, the poems of Julie Fritz offer keen observations on childhood and youth, aging and family. Written with a wry sense of humor and giving Mother Nature a starring role, _Twinings_ is all about making connections."

—Jill McCroskey Coupe, author of
Beginning with Cannonballs

"The immensely gifted painter, Julie Fritz, now frames for us _Twinings_, a lovely late foray of poems suffused with the keenest of light. As in all great landscapes, deity is in the details, and each line, each stroke of the brush as it were, holds illuminative potential."

—Chris Dombrowski, author of
The River You Touch

"A long view, with heart and soul, is what you'll find in this generous collection by a painter turned poet who knows how to look closely and describe what she sees, hears, and feels."

—Holly Wren Spaulding,
author of _Familiars_

Twinings

Poems at Eighty

Julie Fritz

Brandylane
Publishers, Inc.
Publishing books since 1985

Cover art by Julie Fritz

A percentage of sales of this book will go toward research at VCU Massey Cancer Center.

ISBN: 978-1-958754-31-3
Library of Congress Control Number: 2022923512

Designed by Sami Langston
Project managed by Robert Pruett

Printed in the United States of America

Published by
Brandylane Publishers, Inc.
5 S. 1st Street
Richmond, Virginia 23219

brandylanepublishers.com

For my mother, Emily Simpson Paine

CONTENTS

Musings

About the Author

BOOKS BY JULIE FRITZ

Keepers of the Sangres

Remembering a Hill

It is out of the dailiness of life that one is driven into the deepest recesses of the self.

—Stanley Kunitz

Introduction

Breathe it in
and you start to remember
things you didn't know you had forgotten.

                —*Braiding Sweetgrass*
                Robin Wall Kimmerer

My life was not quite a braid. It was not that well thought out. In a way, I just fell through the days spinning, twining, like honeysuckle.

On the little farm where I grew up in East Tennessee, there was an ugly wire fence running across the backyard, keeping the cows on the barn-side from mother's chrysanthemums on the house-side. Over time, honeysuckle covered the fence, turning it into a cushioned chaise lounge where I would settle and read for hours. So, weeds and books intruding on my days have always been a way of life for me. And I think that is why I wrote this book of poems: to tell the story of weeds of all sorts, bumping into us, twining around us and enriching our lives.

MEMORIES

a childhood that never lets go

LUNCH BELL

Mother made me
go outside every morning
if it was above forty-five,
and not come back
until the lunch bell.
I would sit on the terrace
and decide the direction
of the day: south
galloping down gullies
to become Gene Autry
in the High Sierras,
north through the sunken garden,
jousting with trolls
to save the prince,
or west, west to the forbidden lands,
past cows, brambles,
do not trespass signs,
then down, down to Fourth Street Creek.

And it was there I became a poet.

Hunkered, I watched
nubs turning into legs,
striders skating currents,
crawdads cowering in rocks,
caddis flies building castles of sand.

And I never heard the bell.

THE HOGARTH CURVE

It was when I chopped the iris petals,
turned them into ballerina skirts,
and gave dancers pink mimosa hair
that mother sensed the problem.

Still, every June she brought me
into the kitchen to help arrange flowers
for the Sequoia Hills Flower Show,
and it was there we were defined.

It was there the lines were drawn
between precision and exuberance.
As she applied the laws
of focal point and the Hogarth curve,
I dreamily played with ants
coming out of peonies
and tested the taste of petunias.

All of our days
were weighed
in this imbalance,
but we both knew,
for different reasons,
not to use carnations—
and to maintain
the Hogarth curve.

Proper Names

My father told me the names
of the flowers, trees,
birds as we walked lockstep
along worn paths of the Smokies.

Trillium, mayapple, bloodroot,
persimmon, alder, thrasher, thrush.

On the way back to our cabin
I was tested. He said
we owed them that.

Now I still put a name
to all things living,
some correct, some not,
but have yet to find another
to walk the path with me,
the one on the way back.

Attacking Woolworth's Five & Dime

Grandmother shuffled through
the revolving brass doors
of her hotel-home, ready for battle.

Draped in black crepe
loaded with pockets
and locked with buttons,
she marched into Woolworth's Five & Dime.

Her purse, the size of a briefcase,
buckled and zipped, held
Mentholatum, Epsom salts,
Hazel Bishop lipstick,
but no money.

To pay for her Pond's Cold Cream
and my Katy Keene comic books,
Grandmother had to perform an act
sure to embarrass any ten-year-old.

She would bend over,
pull up her skirt,
her petticoats,
and from an elastic garter
holding thick cotton stockings,
unroll the dollar bills
one at a time.

She didn't trust anyone
at Woolworth's Five & Dime.

INTERSTATE 40

Mother stood at the kitchen window
surrounded by linoleum,
looking through lilacs
toward the far Smokies,
but she had no idea
where she was in time.

Between world wars and the Depression,
to the coming of Vietnam,
she stood dangerously in the middle,
wishing only by evening
her husband would drive up
and be content with two Early Times
and a Camel.

But below in the valley
Eisenhower's graders
were smoothing the earth
from St. Louis to Baltimore,
while a daughter
was already questioning
her Bible and Compton's,
and setting in motion
a move up the road.

THE PATH

The cows followed the path
along the hill, zigzagging
to make it easier to get
from fields to barns.

Zigzagging to give them time
to nuzzle the brome,
admire the view.
This I know from watching.

The cows seemed to understand,
as hooves etched the clay,
the gift of the Shenandoah,
the gift of a slow day.

Now those hills are empty
of barns and cows,
while the path still weaves the hill.
This I know from watching.

THE SCREEN DOOR

Summer seemed
to shine on us
when we were young
because of our smallness,
or the clarity of our eyes.

But there were rules.
And the best way to escape
them was to run barefoot
across the gray painted floors
of the wide screened porch
and into the fields.

No one over twelve
would ever follow
or care about us,
as long as we didn't
let the screen door slam.

Sliding Hands

Across the wide cherry table slid
dishes of the fifties,
country-fried steak,
hamburger stroganoff,
tuna casserole.

Sometimes hands from the kitchen
did the sliding;
other times, mother's hands
laid down the plates.

But I knew, even then, with every slide
the two were giving up the original plan—
to serve a greater need
than two children and a man.

GREENHOUSES

My neighbors owned fields
of greenhouses, and somehow
no one minded that I entered at will
to roam the rows, as long as I didn't pick.

Gladiolus, carnations, roses looked down on me,
each specimen dripping a different scent.
If I could have been left alone with them
I would have grown up fearless.

But my brother and his friends from time to time
would decide to play hide-and-seek with me
in those iridescent houses, where there
were a thousand places to hide -
under crates, along banked rows of ferns,
behind hot boilers. I knew them all.

After a while,
hunkering in my perfect spot,
I would begin to realize I was alone.

Everyone else was back at
my house playing Monopoly,
and an emptiness still fills me
from time to time
when I catch the scent of roses.

CANTALOUPES

One slow day every summer,
my neighbor and I
would sneak to the small
house at the back of his
family's sprawling estate
to where the yardman lived.

If his car was not parked
beside the house,
we would run up the steps
onto the front porch,
peek in the window,
open the unlocked front door,
go to the stuffy kitchen,
and find something to destroy.

The best were the cantaloupes.
We would take them
from the windowsill
where they were ripening,
and one-by-one carry them
to the porch and toss each
as hard and far as we could
into the field.

They sailed like flying brains
and smashed to the ground,
splashing orange flesh and seeds
across the alfalfa.

And from then until now,
I have always wondered
why I did that,
because I know,
if I can find an answer,
I can explain evil.

Maroon Cows

Even at ten I knew at night
that the cows had gotten out
by the heavy thunder
beside my open window,
confirmed when I saw maroon
rectangles, big as iceboxes,
bump into one another
next to the lilacs.

It was the fear of every summer.
Tonight, we were at risk
of breaking the county law,
letting livestock run loose
across private properties and highways.

The only hope for all of us,
the whole family,
was to head off the lead
and funnel her into
uneaten pastures.
Afterwards, we went back to sleep,
but I still know that thunder
outside an open window
means trouble.

PEAR TREE

It was just a pear tree,
tall with no spreading canopy,
tall with plain paper petals
and no smell.

It stood beside the toolhouse
forming misshaped ovals
that we assumed would
show up each year
whether we pruned or not.

It must have been planted
by a farmer from Ireland
who failed the land
and moved west.

In October we
broke the hard skins
with our teeth,
sucked the juice,
just like last year,
from a fruit that came too easily,
like a gift unasked for.

PIMENTO CHEESE GLASSES

I tried to carry everything out
before the bulldozers came
but had to think quick
as they climbed the hill
toward our home.

It was hard not to choose
the faux French desk
with sun bleached mahogany
and pink ink stains,
the organdy curtains
still holding summer breezes,
the bent-willow chairs
with canvas cushions remembering
the shape of each aunt,
or those tiny pimento cheese glasses—
the ones with red tulips
stamped around their lip
that held my RC Cola
as I headed to the living room
to watch *Howdy Doody*,
the living room the bulldozers crushed.

MOMENTS

that sometime happen in nature

TWININGS

Sometimes just that
little wisp of honeysuckle,
loaded with nectar,
shooting out the scent of memory
while reaching to twine
with a sister vine,
is the only joy
we are going to get this day.

But we are going to get that.

Just an Old Lady Talking

I know this is just an old lady talking
who has nothing to tell you,
except to mention those blue dahlias
down by the pond that revive themselves
each morning with the sun,
or remind you about that small finch,
the one we didn't think would make it;
he is now awash with purple
and has a song similar to Brahms.

Don't sit with me on the terrace
this evening, you have much to do,
unless you want to taste
the glow given off by the moon
as it nears its fullness,
or listen to the cicadas
on their very best night.

COLUMBINE LEGACY

The columbine
has pushed through peat
for thirty years now,
maybe more,
first purple thumbs,
then clusters
of tissue leaves.

Finally, indigo chandeliers
sway above, long enough
to sow seeds silently
back into the earth,
unaware the planter is dead,
the waterer weak,
and the poet in a garden far away.

ADOLESCENT PEONIES

Just as winter becomes slower,
all quiet and uncomplicated,
in the dark back corner
of the garden
blood red tips show,
so small and raw
they could be
stepped on,
but the swelling
has begun
and there's
no turning back.

No, we must wait
for the rustling
of blush-colored skirts.
We must wait
for our debutantes
to show us
who they want to be.

Before March

Gray sits like a
heavy blanket
across the lumps
of buried perennials.

Sycamores make
no effort toward shade,
geese can't remember
what it feels like to mate
or suck slick grasses.

And me? I too have no memory
of the miracle of March,
so move listlessly from window
to window trying to imagine
what is so special
about forsythia.

EPHEMERALS

Ephemerals are my favorites,
just the sound of the word
sings organdy and chiffon,
too delicate to last
yet determined to push
through deep soil -
blood root, trillium, mayapple.

I wish I were ephemeral
but fear the soil
is too heavy for me.
I'm afraid I only
have one season—
petunia, geranium, zinnia.

ENNUI

Sitting in my tiny yard
nothing has happened
all afternoon,
just over in the blackberry
thicket a family of titmice
attack their next-of-kin while
a late-blooming crabapple
slowly puts out pink.
I try not to move too quickly,
so the dove can continue to nap
while ants move their children
from the chipmunk-destroyed tunnel.
I hope the feet
of my lawn chair
don't squash the roots
of the wisteria
reaching out to the hibiscus,
but I'm not sure,
what with all the rain last night.
Downies crash the suet cage
in their camouflage,
but the jay is not fooled
and spears them away.
The bluebird box
has emptied twice,
giving wasps a chance
to turn pulp to paper.

What a boring,
slow-moving,
nothing-happening
summer afternoon.

Hornworm

Squishing the green globes
sucking my tomato leaves
is the easy part.

As the chartreuse sap runs down my glove
I begin to wonder which butterfly
mothered these worms
and find not a butterfly at all,
but one of my favorite moths,
the hummingbird-look-a-like
hawk moth.

This takes days of weighing
whether or not to kill her babies,
when I learn even more:
an endangered wasp
depends on these juicy backs
to lay its eggs.

Now I'm in a dither
deciding what to do;
squish the destroyer
or the destroyed?

Maybe I should have
spent this much time
on other life choices.

Don't Kill the Badger

Hand-painted signs lined the gravel road,
Don't Kill the Badger.
I was new to rural life
and couldn't get into the mind
of the writer or the reader.

Why would a farmer care about such an ugly animal?
Why would someone waste his rounds on tough meat?

Then I began to fall in love,
as each evening in our front field
a male pulls himself from his den
and lumbers toward prairie dog mounds,
his loose skin undulating over the sage.

His ferocious jaws instantly kill the pups,
taking them gently back to his burrow,
brushing stiff fur against the other badger
before going underground.

FOG

I was beginning to catch
a glimpse of a poem
near the fogged magnolias
at the back of my tiny garden,
beginning to even
pick a perfect word or two
off the misty path
leading there
this morning.

But I fear in a few minutes,
probably less,
the fog will be
sucked away
and the dreamy path
will have turned to crabgrass.

Once again, I have
missed my chance
to tell you something
important, something
to help us both
get back home.

SEED DROP

The purple leaves
at the base of the dogwood
hide the sparrow
catching the seeds
from longer-beaked birds above.

When seed-drop slows
from the feeder,
the sparrow flies up
to see what the hell's going on,
then drops back down
to purple leaves
to think about the distance
between his table and theirs,
between the ground and the feast.

THE SHEDDING

Under the honeysuckle
on sharp curled leaves
I rub back and forth
to slough the skin
that once fit smoothly
but now is
loose,
tattered,
itchy.

Once I had gold flecks
and was desired
in inappropriate ways.
Now bones poke,
breasts sag,
and I only hope
new scales
hurry to hide
my gathering
weakness.

But no, winter comes,
a shortness of breath,
softness in the vertebrae,
and I'm beginning to think
no new skin is going
to bring back summer
or honeysuckle.

FOX CREST

The fox crests snow drifts
like a small red dolphin
breaching waves of white,
swimming closer
and closer to the shore he fears,
crossing the forbidden line
between fescu and terrazzo
to grab the tossed bread
and processed ham,
foods he hates,
then shooting back over the swell
and into a culvert of hard steel
to feed his kits through the cold winter,
colder, he thinks, than before
the humans.

PERIWINKLES

There's no summer
my granddaughters
and I don't collect
handfuls of tiny triangles
lying beside the foam.

The wet miracles
glisten under the sun,
pink, yellow, mauve,
like virgins waiting.

The dull-colored ones
shovel themselves
back into the sand,
but the pretty ones,
the ones we think are girls,
lie open to the sky
until they are chosen.

River Rush

The cloud breaks like glass
and rain fills our mountain pond.
Soon flooding waters start to move
over branch-jammed dams,
through new-carved ravines,
molecule over molecule,
to join the rest of the fast-flowing James.

Currents force the flotilla eastward
along clay-lined banks to the Bay.

At this rate, in ten days the mountain drops
will meet the edge of the ocean
without feeling the softness of mosses,
without hearing the heron's cry.

At this rate, the cycle will run
from beginning to end to beginning
with no reflection
on how to stay still
and be heavy,
on how not to rush
to the cloud.

THREE ORBS ON MY WINDOW

Three orbs attached to a dead leaf
by tender threads of web
carefully placed under its curl,
waiting to let loose,
however tiny, life.

Waiting to slice the shell
and spew into this world
toddlers who fall off tricycles,
teenagers looking for trouble,
disappointed lovers.

Soon spiderlings swirl and cling
for a time, but only a time,
to their mother's filaments
before they realize
they, too, must create orbs
from their innards
and look for a curled leaf
attached to a window.

LOCUST WING FLOATING

Nothing happens
in the garden today
until I fill the fountain
with fresh water
and see floating
a locust wing,
one of a million
I didn't see beating
through the summer.

Just one clear wing,
like a church window
without the stained glass.

MOSS

Everyone tells me I need a purpose,
and I'm sure it's true
that I need to get a foothold
on something meaningful
and move toward it.

But it's sunny today
with a southerly breeze.
Let me lay back
on this soft moss
that has tickled granite
with its tiny roots
for half a billion years.

Red Leaf

Some are amazed
at the red maple leaf,
others the turquoise
lichen bracketing the branch
that holds the leaf.
Me? I caress
the empty scar.

Sparrow, Wren, Thrush

Flitting on the dung-colored leaves
left over from two seasons back
are an assortment of uninteresting birds
using little talon forks to kick up breakfast.

And I am so disappointed in their kind,
the ones given brown feathers
instead of blue or red, colors they
far outnumber. I even wonder
if they have eliminated the pretty ones,
but how could they do that
with short beaks and no weapons?

Then I notice a fleck of yellow on the chipping sparrow,
a slash of purple rising from the finch's brown,
the brown not just brown,
but burnt sienna off the thrush's tail,
orange flicking down the sparrow's back,
the sparrow with yellow eyes and pink beak.

They are all coming to the day just as I do
hesitant, hopeful, and with a slight hop,
awash in color.

CLOUDS OVER MOUNTAINS

The mountains grab
the heavy clouds
like a selfish lover,
not letting them move east,
pulling them close
to suck the soft vapors
deep into the valley
of alfalfa and watercress.

I had always thought power
jumped on top,
now I know it comes
from underneath.

The Concerto

I sit in quietness
near roosting birds
while the wine is still cool.

Then the cicadas,
clinging to a
thousand tiny stages,
begin their concerto,
curving their bodies,
rubbing thighs,
lengthening necks.

And I know,
I know,
today is the day
we are all
at our zenith.

RED BERRIES

When the sun starts to slant
after the sharp rays of summer,
take time to notice the bramble
that shouldered heavy leaves,
see how small red berries
from the bittersweet
now peak into the glow?

While the light is working in our favor,
look at the goldfinch fresh from Maine,
neon feathers ruffled by a far-off front,
black wings curling
the thistle stalk.

Why not let this be your whole afternoon?
Why not let your heart burst like red berries?

But After Winter

We knew we had reached winter
when the trees stopped undressing,
stopped dropping skirts and petticoats
and stood naked and surprised.

All we could now see was bark,
and there is nothing attractive about bark
unless you get close enough to touch it,
unless you run hands over the grey.

But after a cold time in the closet
these trees redress and step out
all green, fresh, and glowing.
That's when the envy begins.

JUST ONE

There was just one,
but that is all it took.
Just one tiny pink butterfly,
like a slip of tissue,
touching down on the only
remaining flower
in the autumn garden,
blooming late,
just to give this wisp
a soft landing.

That's how it is
some mornings.

THE HERON'S HURRICANE

We birds are all atwitter
in the dogwoods
deciding our next move
as the hurricane looms.

Most are catching the
updraft to flee, but down below,
the heron with iron feathers
is my biggest concern.

She hasn't moved the
whole summer, ever since I arrived,
so how is this wrought wader
going to escape cruel winds?

I whisper to her,
coax her, but her talons
are grounded in mulch,
her wings tight by her side.

Slowly it's coming to me,
as first bands circle the sky,
I only have one choice—
I have to stand by.

So I'll stay in this coastal garden
alone with my heavy burden
and always, always wonder;

did she worry about me?

FLOW FROM FLOWERS

To make a pound of honey, bees have to gather
nectar from two million flowers.
  —Canadian Honey Council

At first, I thought the sound
came from the garden,
but it was louder at night,
like little violins,
the hum swelling
through our house.

Then the ooze began,
a slow gathering of amber
seeping through
cabbage rose wallpaper,
under oak moldings
and onto my daughter's
bedroom floor.

To me it was a miracle
gathered from a thousand fields,
to my daughter it was a devastation,
a portent of ruptures to come.

MUSINGS

from the wisdom age gifts us

WHAT IF

I fear that I am different
from most people.
Maybe everyone
wants to sit and think about Mary Oliver
poems and stand close to a tree trunk
to see how many colors they can find
on the bark and wonder how many heart
beats they have left in a lifetime
and why oceans stop where they do.

But what if they don't?

POSTCARD TO MY FORMER SELF

Good to hear from you after so many seasons,
I often wonder how you are. I am
splendid, though a hip gives me a shuffle,
and your silky hair has coarsened,
but that means I now have curls.

I remember you had dreams, soft,
sensual ones, while mine now
solve problems for ten or so
descendants, but I sleep until five
and am still content with instant coffee.

Glad to hear you have a new boyfriend
and exceptional birds at your feeder.
Not sure how to respond, knowing what I know,
but I will say my birds are all
the same color and heading south soon.

Too bad we can't meet halfway
for wine—maybe St. Louis,
but, of course, we can't, what with
time zones and your schedule, still know
I am always proud of who you became.

THE WOMEN ARTISTS OF MONHEGAN ISLAND

Artists don't like to organize,

but the men on the island,

the artist men,

were taking up all the space

in the books and the galleries,

so the women artists,

and there were many,

carried casseroles and canvases

to a porch overlooking

the crashing Atlantic

and claimed their place,

The Women Artists of Monhegan Island,

and proceeded to paint rocks and waves

and fields as only women can—

with a passion in their stroke

that pulls from the womb

past the heart on its way

to the fingertips,

the ones tasting of

chicken broth and thyme.

Waiting for Wine

The thirst starts at three
to pour the wine,
but first the cardinals
must rise to the shoulders
of the rhododendron,
the lichen on the ash
sink into shadow,
and the lights
at each window
across the street
come on
before I sip.

Have I answered the questions
that rose with the sun?
Have I quelled my fears
of the future,
put order back
in the garden?
Do the grandchildren
still think I'm funny
and doctors give
me more time?

By five, the answers are mixed
while the wine still holds its chill.

Now I See

The grandmother I didn't know,
the paternal one, who
used to hum and smile and sit
softly on any cushioned chair,
her layered floral dress
matching the chintz so well
she was camouflaged
throughout the day.

I thought she had a
weakness, a disease,
but now I see
she, like me,
was happy with the way things
had turned out, the way life
had placed her on a soft cushion.

So now I hum.

Letting Go

The bur oak has let loose
most of its leaves;
maybe two piles worth
still hold to branches
like cranky old ladies
waiting for their tea.

But those ladies don't look
scared or shattered
and when they drop,
they don't seem to suffer,
they just let go,
a whoosh of soft wind
and a letting go.

CARRYING CASSEROLES

We thought miniskirts and vinyl boots
and the smooth flow of Crosby, Stills & Nash
would get us through the choices we made,
believed carrying casseroles
across shag rugs assured
our lives would be as good,
maybe even better, than our parents,
forgetting we were carrying husbands
who had not been schooled
in the final chapters
of Betty Friedan.

NEXT YEAR

I promise next year
to curry your stems, ruffle your mulch,
nurse your roots with water,
unlike this summer
when I stalked the only available male
on our cul-de-sac and spent too much time
holding my wine to the sun
looking for slow moving light.

I am sorry I maybe caused your wilt,
but that is not why finches
no longer come.

AT MY AGE

At my age I should know
what time the sun changes
the shape of the cedars
and which night the full moon
surprises the sky.

I should know
answers to children's questions
like why hollyhocks
don't last forever
and spring comes
just once a year.

Yet at my age
I only understand
tiny thoughts,
the softness of sheets,
the gift of candlelight.
I'll have to wait
till I'm older
for the big answers.

JUNE 1

Summer's soft shoulders
have begun to lean
into the scent of jasmine
while nightgowns and
blankets slide from the bed,
all heaviness gone.

Somehow the slant
of the sun pinpoints us
in the universe
as if we were the chosen,
but just for a while,
before the tilt back.

And it is now, quickly, we have
to work our juices to the top
like the beebalm, the phlox,
and show the world
we have more than one color
and maybe some seeds.

WINGED WOMEN

Today in West Palm Beach
a seventy-year-old woman fell
from her ninth-floor balcony
onto an awning.

Unhurt.

I can easily see it happening.
She was spring cleaning
her three- by nine-foot walled terrace,
compacting into that small space.

A ritual of spring.

Forcing onto that narrow ledge
the rite of seventy other springs
in fields and woods and lawns
far away from West Palm Beach.

Of course she fell off!

It's amazing there aren't
seventy-year-old women
flying off balconies
all over the world.

On a pretty spring day.

THE CONSIGNMENT

I take them out of the closet
deciding the fate of each,
knowing the life they decorated
is now out of reach.

They have hung here for years,
too precious to give away,
but we're downsizing the house
and besides—they've had their day.

Yet these artifacts have been with me
for, what, thirty years?
Is it really time to give them up,
to accept my greatest fears?

That romance can't be clothed,
that dances aren't still to be danced,
that I won't need a de la Renta.
that I won't have another chance.

Wait, these are works of art
adorned with filigrees
draped on the bias
with way too many memories.

A gown shared a dinner in Paris,
one was ripped while in Palm Beach,
the peignoir caught perfumed air
on a yacht near Bitter Reach.

Oh, there's still too much life in them,
I can hear the sway and swoon.
I can remember them hugging my body
when a man looked across the room.

So I lay them on the bed by season,
assessing their secondhand chance,
knowing they are passé
but not too old to dance.

Yet the cute young appraisers
will only see moth holes and crinkles,
will frown at the choice of colors
and deduct for stains and wrinkles.

They will see relics of the '80s
and assign them to the very last rack,
while I still see silk and velvet
and still feel a breath on my back.

OLD GRAY CEMETERY

Each time I come
to Old Gray Cemetery
it seems to shrink.

Once a wide sweep of moss
holding my mother, my father,
a grandmother, each comfortable and content,
I think, inside the wrought iron fence.

Now I can hardly step without insulting
a brother, two aunts, an ex-sister-in-law
layered long this way and that, still content,
I think, inside the wrought iron fence.

But this plot needs to fit one more,
and I have been told I have a chance,
at the foot of my father, twelve-by-twelve
inches I think, inside the wrought iron fence.

The Retirement Home

She made her way
through summer air
amid hostas and bee balm,
under a loose windowsill
and into the cool house.

Weaving her web
between chair leg and table,
then snuggling into the base
of the Hepplewhite,
she was finally set for the fall.

When the movers came all seemed normal;
the Hepplewhite was wrapped in pads,
carefully loaded on the truck
and professionally placed in the condo.

Up fifteen floors,
overlooking the ocean,
near a wide window
but still attached to the Hepplewhite,
she was safe and secure.

The spider went about her daily routine,
reweaving, cleaning, preparing for the night,
then swinging to the center
when the sun went down.
waiting for crickets and mites.

Each day she remembered the woods
where the smell of earth prevailed,
summer rains that threatened to drown,
winds that scattered her brood.
She remembered the life she loved.

Each day she watched the ocean,
the smooth spread of waves on the beach,
she languished in this sun-drenched beauty,
a beauty with no hostas or crickets.

MATRIARCHS AT THE BEACH

All up and down the Atlantic coast
and probably the Pacific,
old mothers, grandmothers really,
are driving, or being driven,
to moldy, unacceptable beach houses
to gather their progeny together
one more time, one more summer,
knowing from the first toss
of sheets onto rented beds,
this might not work.

Matriarchs finally,
they experiment with a power
they have never had before,
never really wanted,
and by the time
the first gin and tonic
is poured there's
a little unrest amongst
the sisters on the porch.

This has to happen all
up and down the seaboard,
like a million butterfly wings
atwitter at once,
causing the salt air
to stir with a foreboding sense—
this will be a long week.

FIGURINES

On the walnut whatnot
in the corner,
mother touched
the delicate people,
proud of their elegance.

She fingered their porcelain
like a child,
smoothing the ladies' ruffles,
clicking the men's high heels,
proud of their linage
and pastel colors,
the colors of her bathrobe.

On their underside
were taped little
folded messages;
where they were bought,
where they were to go.

And we never knew
what to do
with them,
or the whatnot,
or mother.

To Calm Cattle

It takes skill to calm cattle.

First, find fresh, tasseling alfalfa,
blow its pollen toward the oldest mother,
the one who has been open for three years
but still yearns for birth and will listen to you.

The sun needs to be high,
when the meadowlarks are napping
and before the red-tail circles.

Get closer, breathe toward her ear
but breathe softly—
she knows what sorrow you carry
and will let go her fear
to keep you from the edge,
to keep you calm.

TUMBLER

It seems
I keep revisiting my past
in journal after journal
trying to come
to some conclusion
and all I really do
is tumble
over and over
the rocks of my life
rendering them
smaller and
smaller.

THE LAST BEACH WALK

We have to step tender down
dunes while sea oats recover
and turtle eggs hold whole.

Arm folded into the crook of her elbow,
I am where I have wanted to be
for sixty years.

Finally, we are casting similar
shadows as foam licks our feet,
and we each loosen our grip
on the past that held us tight.

Further down the beach,
where waves shimmer violet,
I remember why I am here—
to put my arm around her cold shoulders
and tell her I love her
for the first time
while sandpipers
kiss the salt.

ABOUT THE AUTHOR

Julie Plunkett Fritz has been known as a marketing consultant and abstract landscape artist. But now at eighty, she will be known as a poet, with her first book of published poems, *Twinings*. She grew up on a small farm in East Tennessee, raised her family in Richmond, Virginia, then lived in varied lands throughout the country just to see what they were like—after first checking them out on the back of a motorcycle! She now lives quietly with her husband back in Richmond, Virginia.